VEHICLES ON THE JOB

EXCAVATORS

ON THE CONSTRUCTION SITE

by Samantha Bell

Cherry Lake Press

Published in the United States of America
by Cherry Lake Publishing
Ann Arbor, Michigan
www.cherrylakepublishing.com

Reading Adviser: Beth Walker Gambro, MS, Ed., Reading Consultant, Yorkville, IL
Content Adviser: Louis Teel, Professor of Heavy Equipment Operating, Central Arizona College

Photo Credits: © Maksim Safaniuk/Shutterstock, © aleksej015/Shutterstock, cover, title page; © ABCDstock/Shutterstock, 4; © XooKits/Shutterstock, 6; © photoschmidt/Shutterstock, 8; © Another77/Shutterstock, 10; © Dusan Petkovic/Shutterstock, 12; © Roman Vasilenia/Shutterstock, 14; © Ralf Geithe/Shutterstock, 16; © Taras Verkhovynets/Shutterstock, 18; © Kletr/Shutterstock, 20

Cherry Lake Press is an imprint of Cherry Lake Publishing Group.

Library of Congress Cataloging-in-Publication Data has been filed and is available at catalog.loc.gov

Cherry Lake Press would like to acknowledge the work of the Partnership for 21st Century Learning, a Network of Battelle for Kids. Please visit Battelle for Kids online for more information.

Printed in the United States of America

Note from Publisher: Websites change regularly, and their future contents are outside of our control. Supervise children when conducting any recommended online searches for extended learning opportunities.

TABLE OF CONTENTS

MADE FOR THE JOB SITE

An **excavator** looks like a huge shovel on a machine. It has a large bucket. It has a long **boom**.

LOOK

Look at the boom. It has a joint like an elbow. How could this help it do its job?

Some excavators move on wheels. Some move on **tracks**. They can do many different jobs.

TAKING TURNS

The **operator** sits in the excavator. This area is called a cab. The cab can turn in a circle.

CONNECT

What other vehicles have cabs?

The operator turns the cab around. The operator can see everything at the **site**.

DIG IT, LOAD IT

Excavators can dig large holes. They dig out basements for homes. They dig **trenches** for pipes.

2000
221

They load the dirt into dump trucks. The trucks take it away.

POWER MOVES

Excavators can lift heavy things. They lift heavy pipes and huge rocks.

They can knock down buildings.
They can cut and break buildings.

THINK

Why do you think a building might need to be knocked down?

Excavators are powerful machines!

FIND OUT MORE

Go online with an adult to find videos of excavators. Write down some things you **see** and **hear**.

Then, write what you **think** about those things. **Make a connection** to something else you know.

Next, write what you **wonder** about excavators from the videos. What would you like to learn more about?

GLOSSARY

boom (BOOM) the long, arm-like part that is used to lift and move the bucket

excavator (EK-skuh-vay-tor) a machine that prepares the ground for constructing a building

operator (AH-puh-ray-tur) someone who works a machine

site (SITE) the place where something was, is, or will be built

tracks (TRAKS) the metal or rubber belts on a vehicle that make it move

trenches (TRENCH-ez) long, narrow holes in the ground

INDEX

ABOUT THE AUTHOR

Samantha Bell has written over 100 books for children. She lives in South Carolina with her family and pets.